DRAWING HALLOWEEN

Halloween, on the 31st of October, is the night when weird, creepy, spine-tinglingly, spooky things happen.

Tradition tells us that witches take to their broomsticks to fly through starry autumn skies, cackling and screaming, while their black cats hold on tight.

It is the night that werewolves roam, baying at the moon, when the ghosts of those that lived long ago, wander lonely paths and corridors, seeking their lost lives, loves and hopes, before fading into the early-morning mists for another year.

Beware the vampires, for this is the night they search for fresh blood. And keep careful watch for trick-or-treaters, creeping through the streets, calling on unsuspecting neighbours.

Have lots of candy ready or face the consequences!

Stay inside and draw. It's the safest thing to do!

Happy Halloween Drawing!

PUMPKINS

SIMPLE LIT PUMPKIN FACE

1. Sketch the outline shape in pencil.
2. Create a cut-in shape for the stalk.
3. Draw the stalk and face.
4. Add extra lines for thickness of skin.

OPEN LIT PUMPKIN FACE

1. Sketch pumpkin shape, with oval at the top, to create outline for the opening. 2. Sketch lines towards centre as guides and draw the face. 3. Draw curves around the hole and add extra lines to create the thickness of the skin - erase pencil guides.

PUMPKIN LEAF

1. Sketch five lines in a star-shape for the veins. 2 Draw circles in between the veins and curves around line ends. 3. Connect the circles and the curves to create the leaf outline. 4. Add the stalk and extra veins - erase pencil guides.

PUMPKIN TENDRIL

1. Pencil-in three circles and connect them along top as if looping.
2. Sketch the second row of loops. 3. Ink the drawing. 4. Add shading.

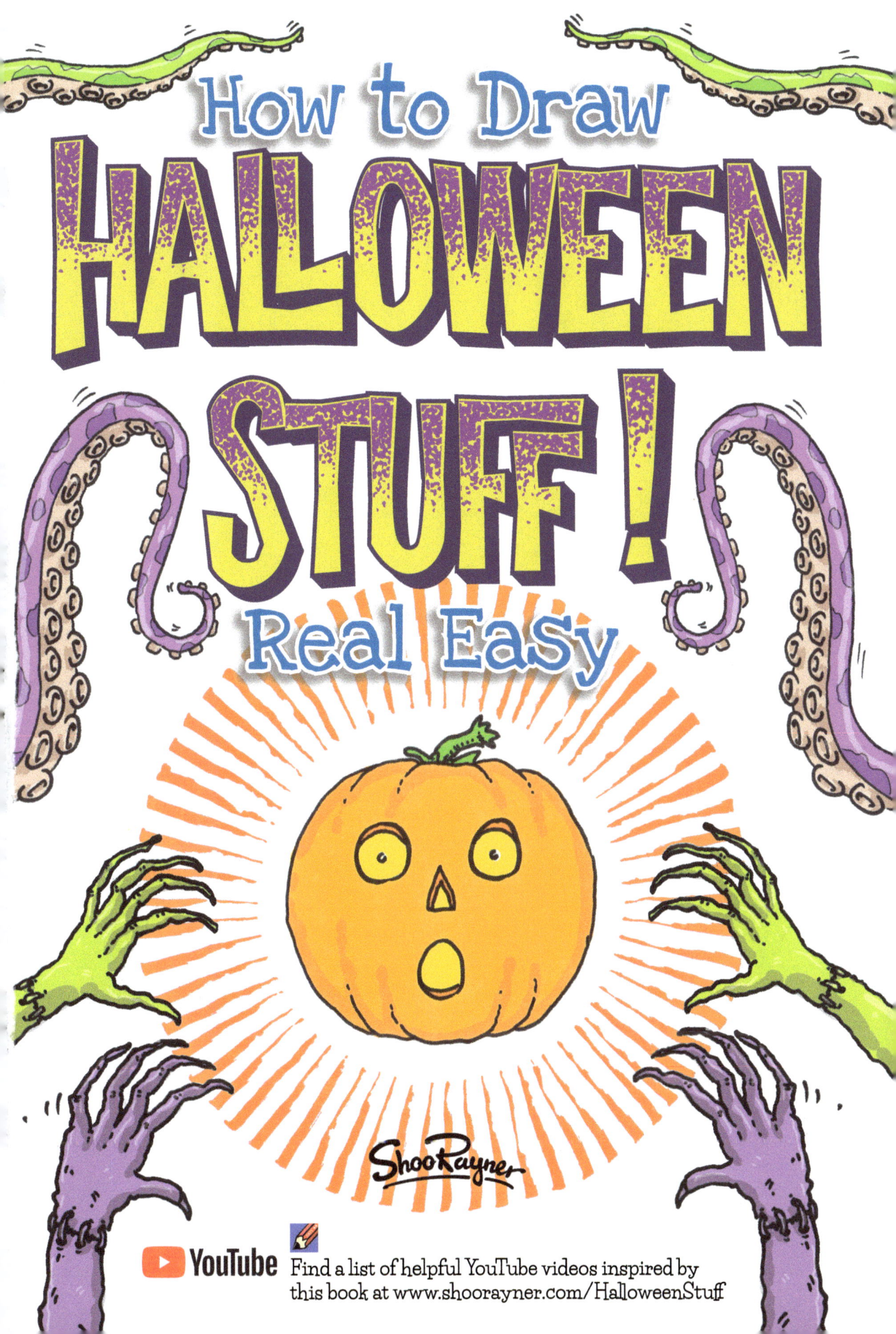

How to Draw
HALLOWEEN STUFF!
Real Easy

ShooRayner

 **YouTube** Find a list of helpful YouTube videos inspired by this book at www.shoorayner.com/HalloweenStuff

Published by Shoo Rayner

www.shoorayner.com

ISBN 978-1-908944-43-6

Text and illustrations
© Shoo Rayner 2021

A CIP catalogue record for this book is
available from the British Library.

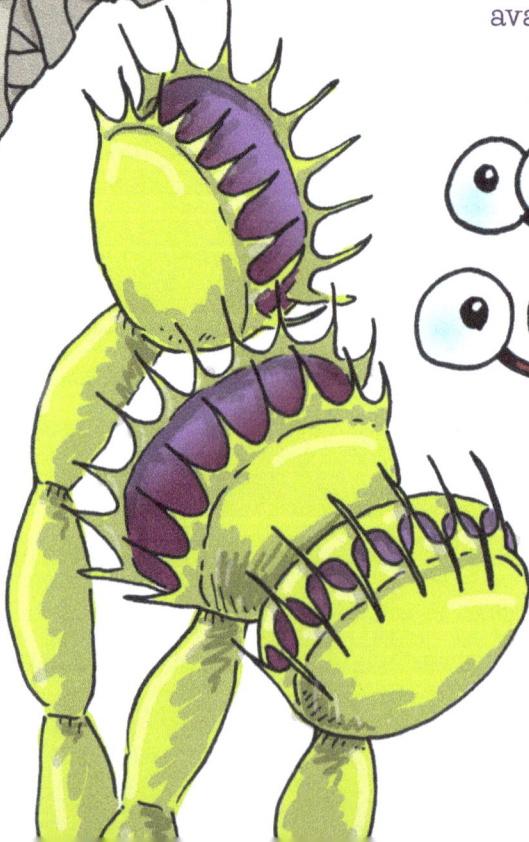

PUMPKIN FACES

24 designs to frighten-up the neighbourhood!

WITCHES

WITCH'S HEAD

1 begin by sketching a circle for the head and an oval for the hat brim. Add the pointy part on top.

2. Draw the hat band and buckle, then draw the face (See how it follows the circle.) Begin to draw hair.

3. Add centre of buckle, evil eye, teeth and finish the rest of the hair.

FLYING WITCH

1. Sketch the basic curve and the line for broomstick - (the red line) then outline the basic shapes for the flying witch.

2. Draw the outline of the cat sitting on the broom - there are more detailed cat drawings over the page. Draw the cloak and the hands.

3. Draw the witch's dress, adding fold details.
Then draw the boots, broomstick and a worried expression on the cat's face!

STARS

1. Fill the night sky with stars.

2. Draw up & down to make a "mountain."

3. Draw a line across and 3. Join points.

Thin Star.

Thick Star.

WITCHY STUFF

POINTY WITCH HAT

Witches' hats can be simple and pointy or a bit old and battered.

1. Begin by sketching an oval with a triangle on top.
2. Draw a curve at the bottom of the triangle.
3. Add another curve above for hat band and add the buckle.

OLD WITCH'S HAT

1. Draw this the same way, as the pointy hat, but fold the top of the point over. 2. Put some kinks in it, adding extra lines to accentuate the folds. Draw buckle. 3. Draw hat band and draw the brim, making it look old with a jaggy, shaky line.

BROOMSTICK

1. Sketch the outline of the handle and the brush in pencil., 2. Ink in the handle and the brush ties. 3. Then draw the brush end, using either a simple straight style or a more pointy "paintbrush" style.

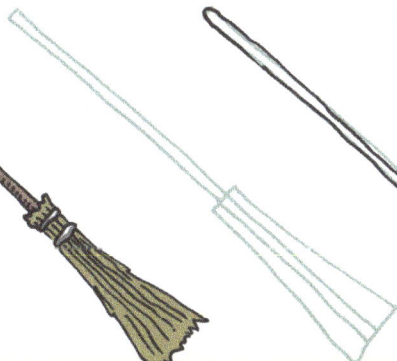

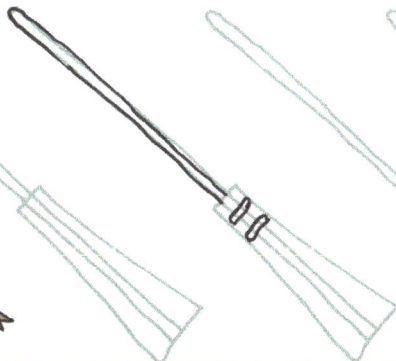

BLACK CATS

LYING CAT

1. Sketch the basic shapes in pencil - Circle for head and sausage for the body. 2. Draw the outline, adding a collar to join head to body. 3. Finish with the face, paws and don't forget the whiskers!

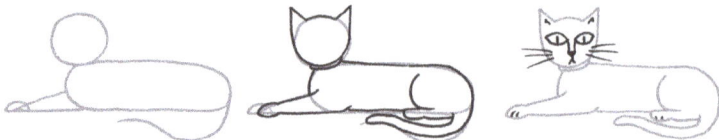

SITTING CAT

1. Sketch the body shapes in pencil 2. Draw the head. Connect to body with a collar. Draw the back and curl it around into the tail. 3. Add legs and paws. 4 Finish with face and whiskers.

SPITTING CAT

1. Sketch the body shapes in pencil
2. Draw the head, then the arched back with fur sticking up and top of tail. Draw backs of legs.
3. Draw eyebrows, nose and hissing mouth shape. Finish legs and tail.
4. Finish angry face and add angry motion marks.

WALKING CAT

1. Sketch the body shapes in pencil 2. Draw the head, connect to the body with a collar. Draw the back and tail. Draw backs of legs and curve of thigh 3. Add face and whiskers. Finish legs and add "tail wags".

WITCH'S CAULDRON

1. Draw an oval for the top and then the round belly of the pot with triangle legs below. 2. Add curve for mouth of pot and handles on the sides. 3. Draw handle rings, bubbles and then the liquid level. 4 Finish with shading.

MAGIC SPELL BOOK

1. A book is basically a box. Start by sketching a parallelogram.
2. Pencil the spine of the book and the pages. Add curves on spine.
3. Draw outline of book in "old" shaky lines. Add curves on spine.
4. Add cover fold line, details on spine and cover image.
   Draw the pages and the book band that holds pages together.
5. Write "SPELLS" on cover and add more decoration

SPELLS

Cast your spells with these magic spell effects - how to draw a wand overleaf.

ZAP!   **SPIRAL**   **FLAME**   **GLITTER**

SPELLS

MAGIC POTION

1. Plan the bottle shape in pencil and ink the bottom half.
2. Draw the potion liquid inside.
3. Draw a cork in the bottle neck plus some shiny reflection in the glass.
4. Finish off by designing your own magic label.

MAGIC LOVE POTION

1. Plan the bottle shape in pencil
2. Draw the bottle outline.
3. Draw the base of the bottle.
4. Draw the magic liquid.
5. Draw the shadows and highlights.

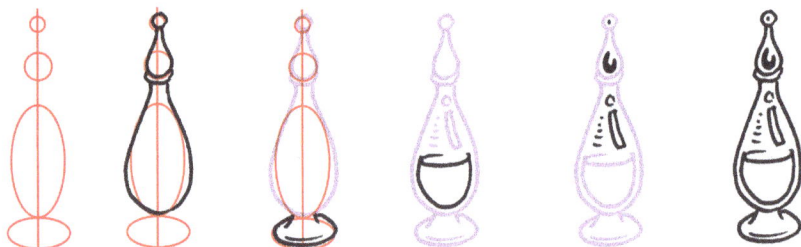

STAR MAGIC WAND

1. Sketch line. 2. Ink in arrow for bottom of star and jewel at base of handle. 3. Draw handle and wand shaft. 4. Draw star at top and make it sparkle!

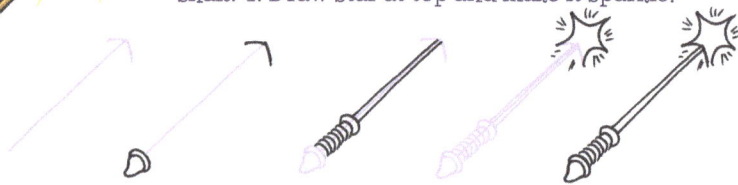

SPIRAL MAGIC WAND

1. Sketch a wiggly line. 2. Draw jewel at base of handle. 3. Draw spirals. (Each spiral is like a "S" shape". 4. Continue spirals to a point and add magic "crackles"

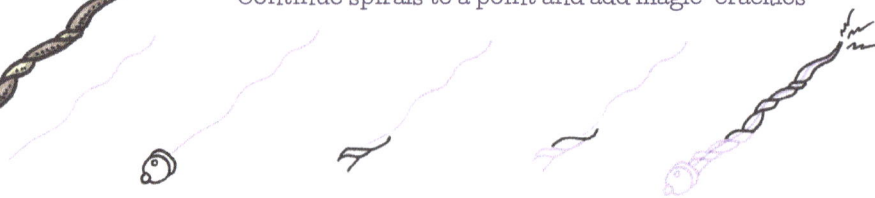

SKULLS

HUMAN SKULL FRONT VIEW

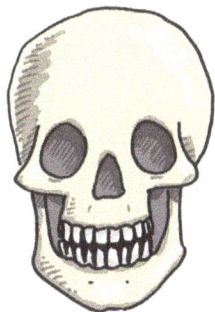

1. Sketch the outline plan and draw eye and nose sockets. 2. Draw cheeks and top gum. 3. Draw lower jaw and teeth. 4. Draw top of skull slightly larger than the circle on plan. 5. Add shading.

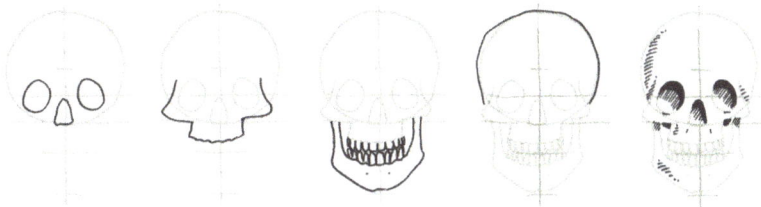

HUMAN SKULL SIDE VIEW

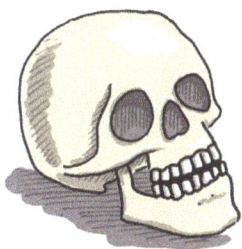

1. Sketch the outline plan and draw eye and nose sockets and draw round the top of the skull. 2. Draw cheeks, jaw and teeth then 3. Finish with shading.

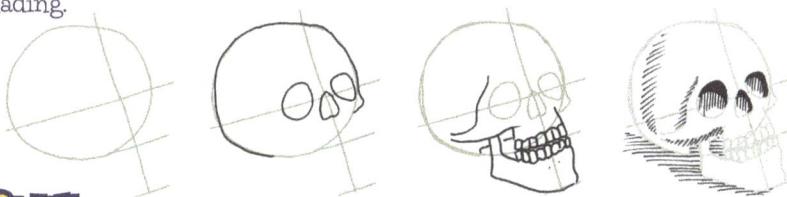

LAUGHING SKULL

1. Sketch the outline plan and draw eyes and nose. 2. Draw cheeks, jaw and teeth then 3. Draw lower jaw and top of skull then 4. Finish with shading.

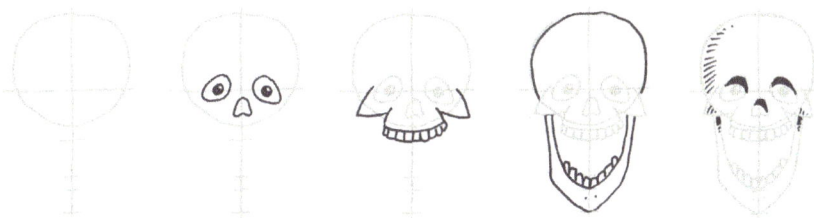

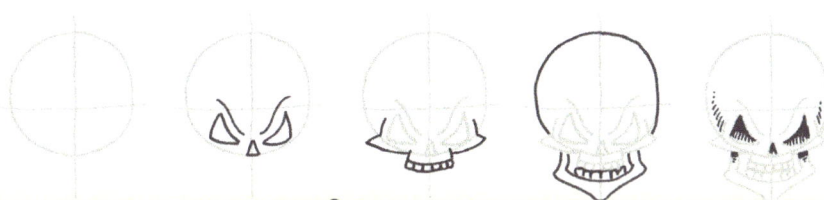

SCARY SKULL

1. Sketch the outline plan and draw eyes and nose. 2. Draw cheeks, jaw and teeth then 3. Draw lower jaw and top of skull then 4. Finish with shading.

HUMAN SKELETON

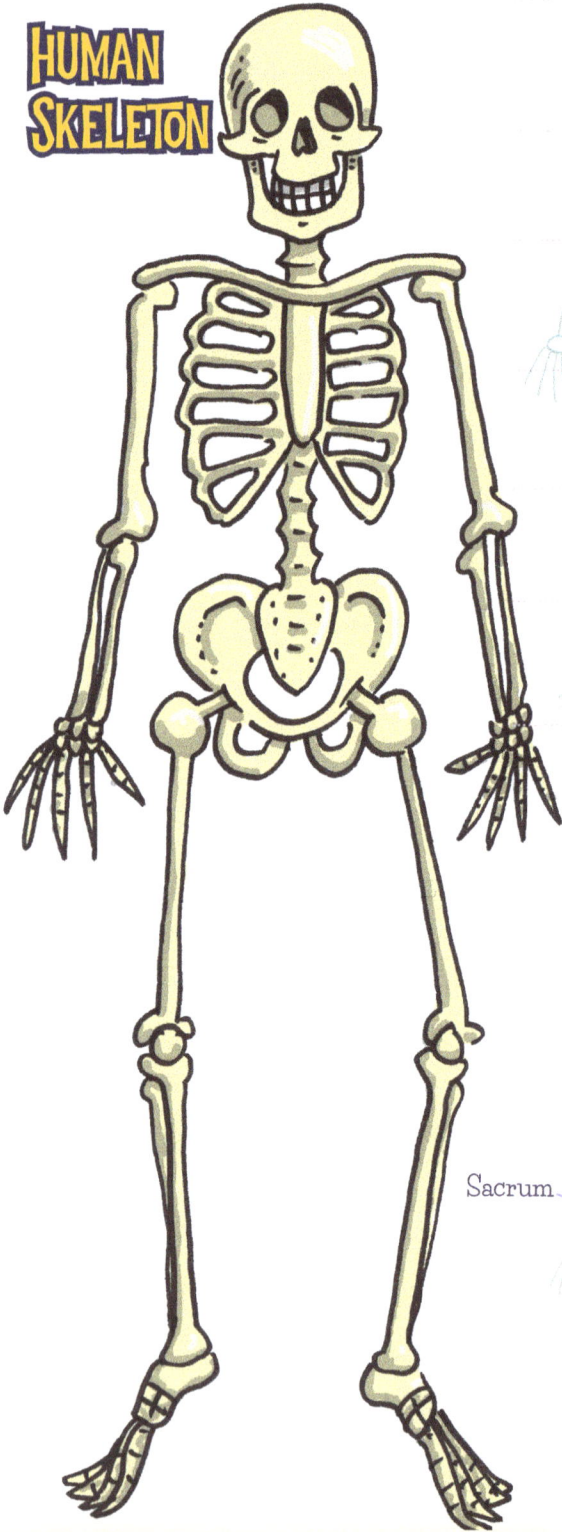

1. Begin by sketching a plan in pencil.

2. Draw the skull - see previous page - then draw neck and shoulders. Then draw thigh bones in pelvis.

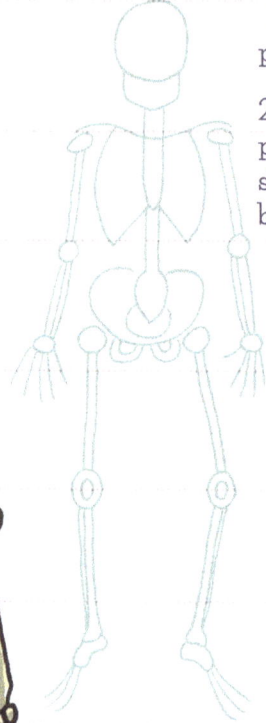

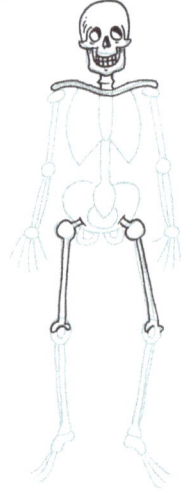

3. Draw sternum, backbone and sacrum, then upper arm bones and knee caps.

4. Draw hands, ribs, upper part of pelvis, then lower leg bones.

5. Finish with lower part of pelvis and foot bones.

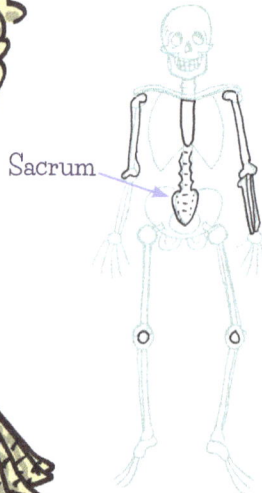

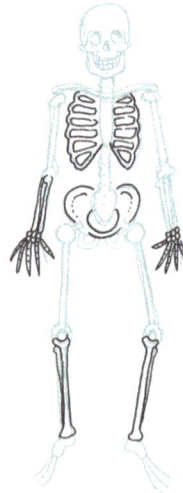

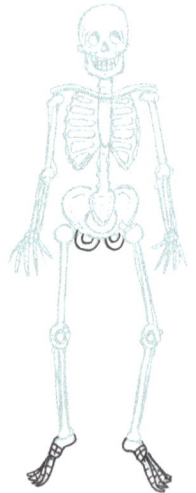

Sacrum

EYE BALLS

STARING GLASS EYE

1. Begin by sketching a plan in pencil - it's all circles!

2. Draw the pupil and iris lines radiating outwards. Draw shadow in one direction then 3. Cross-hatch in the opposite direction

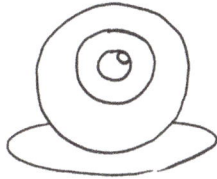

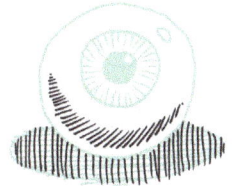

GLOOPY EYE

1. Begin by sketching a plan in pencil - it's all circles again!

2. Ink the eyeball and draw the dome of gloopiness.

3. Ink the iris lines and gloopiness.

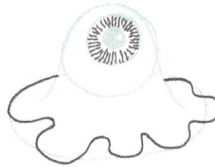

4. Draw the shading

SEVERED EYE

Complete with Optic Nerve.

1. Begin by sketching a plan in pencil - circles like before - then add wiggly lines for the Optic Nerve.

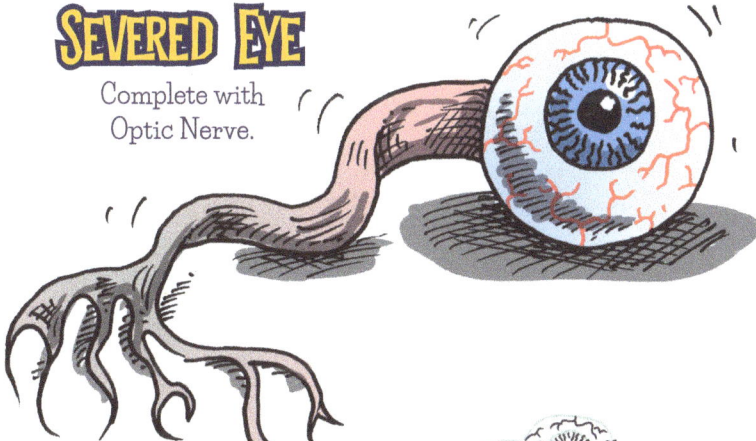

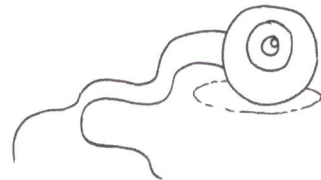

2. Ink in the eyeball, veins and fibres of the Optic Nerve.

3. Ink in the shading.

HORRIBLE HANDS

SEVERED HAND

1. Begin by sketching a plan in pencil.

2. In ink, draw the outlines of lower sides of fingers and top of thumb - hook around the finger tips.

3. Draw top outlines of fingers and thumb and ragged severed edge.

4. Add palm creases shading and twitch marks.

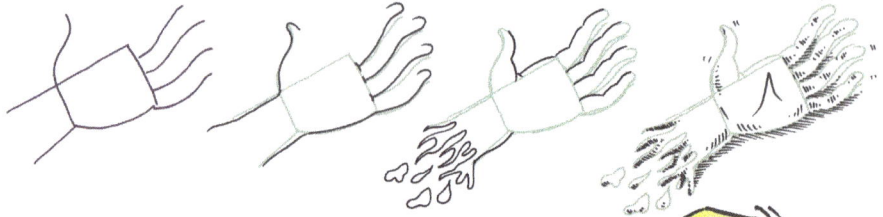

CREEPY HAND

1. Begin by sketching a plan in pencil.

2. In ink, draw the nails then 3. Draw the outlines of fingers, thumb, wrist and arm.

4. Draw hairy bits, shading and shiver marks.

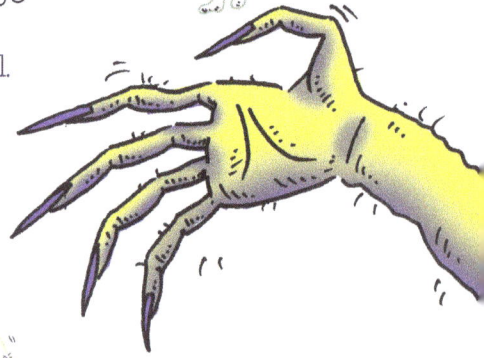

SKELETON HAND

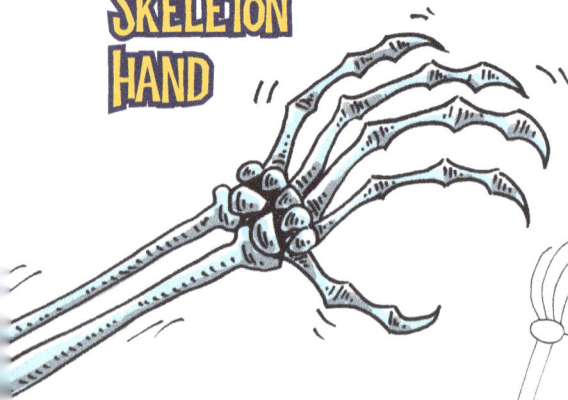

1. Begin by sketching a plan in pencil.

2. In ink, draw the wrist and arm bones

3 and 4 - draw outlines of fingers and thumb .

5. Add shading and shaking marks.

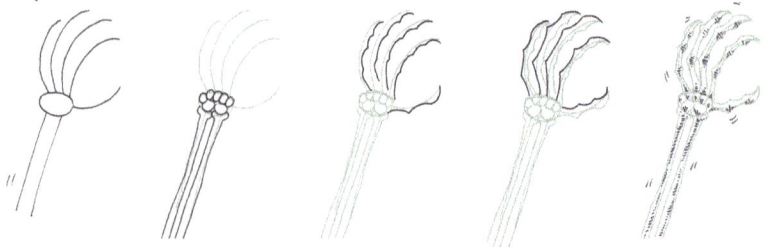

BATS

SCARY BAT

1. Sketch a cross in pencil - draw it at an angle.

2. Ink top of head and curves of tops of wings.

3. Draw curves to complete wings, meeting at a point at the tail.

4. Draw eyes just below horizontal of cross point and add "flight marks".

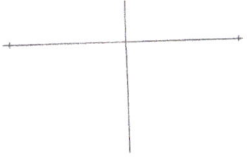

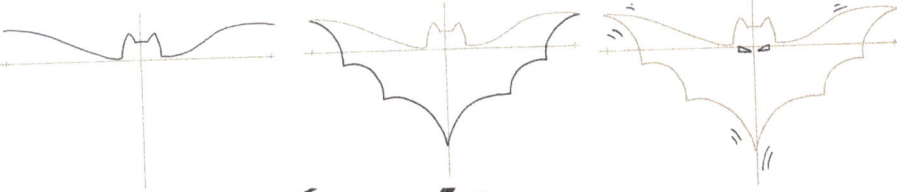

UPSIDE DOWN BAT

1. Sketch a branch and oval for body in pencil.

2. Ink branch, ears and tops of wings.

3. Draw curves to complete wings.

4. Draw eyes, legs, furry body and "fingers", then add "shake marks".

CUTE BAT

1. Sketch a cross in pencil. Draw it at an angle and sketch oval for body shape.

2. Ink top of head and curves of tops of wings.

3. Draw curves to complete wings, and finish lower body.

4. Draw eyes on horizontal of cross. Draw legs and add "flight marks".

Draw a circle to make a moon.

FACES OF FEAR!

HOME ALONE!

1. Sketch an oval in pencil then, 2. Draw the hair.

3. Draw eyes with worried eyebrows, nose, ears. Draw mouth open, to show bottom row of back teeth and tongue.

4. Finish with extra hair marks, ear holes and shoulders.

1. Pencil an oval and outlines for hair and kneck, then, 2. Draw the fringe, face, nose, ear and mouth outlines in ink.

3. Draw eyes with worried eyebrows and finish hair then, 4. Finish mouth and neck before adding marks of fear!

IT'S BEHIND YOU!

 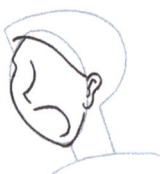   

SHOCK HORROR!

1. Pencil an oval for the face then 2. Draw the shoulders and head outline, including ears.

3. Draw eyes, eyebrows, nose and open mouth then, 4. Draw hair, lips, tongue and creases either side of nose. Finish with marks of fear!

1. Pencil a pointed oval for the face then 2. Draw the hair, shoulders and chin.

3. Draw eyes with worried eyebrows, nose and open mouth then, 4. Finish with hair, teeth and wiggly lines of fear!

QUIVER & QUAKE

POSES OF FEAR!

THE SCRUNCH

1. Sketch the outline plan in pencil,

2. Draw the hair and hands.

3. Draw eyes with worried eyebrows, nose, and open mouth.

4. Finish with clothes, make sure to draw "behind" fingers.

1. Sketch the outline plan in pencil,

2. Draw the face outline, hair and hands.

3. Draw eyes with worried eyebrows, nose, and open mouth. Then draw the jeans.

4. Finish with shoes, T-shirt and scare marks.

THE BIG TRIP

GRRRRRRR!

1. Sketch the outline plan in pencil,

2. Draw the hair, face outline, v-shaped eyebrow and hands.

3. Draw eyes, nose, open mouth and T-shirt.

4. Finish with leggings, shoes and scare marks..

SCARY STICKMEN

Stick people are easy to draw and are great for sketching poses of fear.

Draw a stick person pose in pencil and use it as a frame to build a drawing on top.

Ink the sketch then erase the pencil to reveal a clean, finished drawing.

Surprise!

Zombie

Not me!

Whaaah?

OMG!

Mercy!

Please, no!

Keep back!

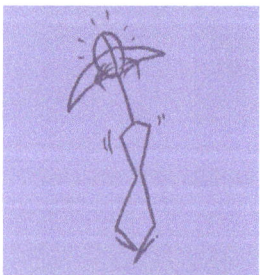

Wobbly knees!!

Tense

Whassup!

What was that?

Against the wall

Begging

Run!

Stay there!

SPRIGHTLY SPOOKS

BLOB

1. Sketch the outline plan in pencil then, 2. Draw the left hand curve then, 3. The right hand curve. 4. Draw eyes across middle line and mouth below. Add wobble marks.

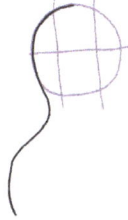

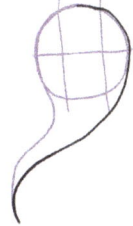

DRIP

1. Sketch the outline plan in pencil then, 2. Add drips either side of middle drip then, 3. Add outside drips and draw all around top of head. 4. Draw eyes, mouth and wobble marks.

DRIBBLE

1. Sketch the outline plan in pencil then,
2. Draw hands and top of head. Add eyes and mouth then,
3. Draw left hand side and then,
4. Right hand side and add wobble marks.

BLOOP

1. Sketch the outline plan in pencil then,
2. Draw round top of head and shoulders,
3. Draw the "skirts from the armpits.
4. Draw eyes, mouth and satisfaction marks.

FRIGHTENING PHANTOMS

BOO!

1. Sketch the outline plan in pencil, with the two circles representing the palms of the hands.

2. Draw the hat and curve lines up to the thumbs. Draw the bottom wiggly line.

3. Complete thumbs and first fingers, then draw folds of the hat and bottom of body.

4. Finish the hands and arms, then draw eyes and scary mouth.

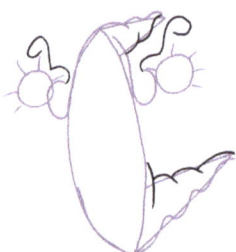

SCREAMER

1. First draw the outline in pencil, then...

2. Draw the skull outline first, then inner cowl, eyes and screaming mouth.
Last, draw outer cowl or hood.

3. Draw wings in tatters and,
4. Finish body with tattered skirts at the bottom.

COFFINS

HOW TO DRAW A BOX

1 Begin by drawing a long parallelogram, then, 2. Draw another vertically downwards at one end, then 3. Finish with another vertical at the end and join at the bottom of the box.

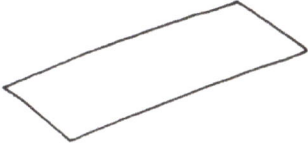
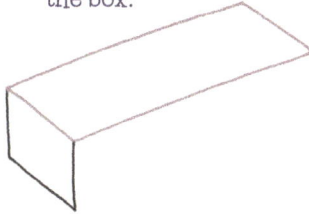
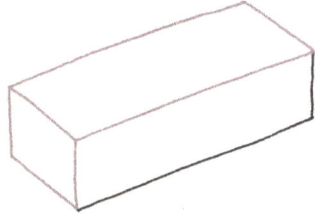

PINE BOX

1. First, sketch a box for an outline plan to help you sketch the coffin shape.

2. Draw the lid with nameplate and closing screws.

3. Draw vertical lines to create the sides and draw the lip of the bottom moulding.

4. Finish up with the handles and the rest of the bottom moulding.

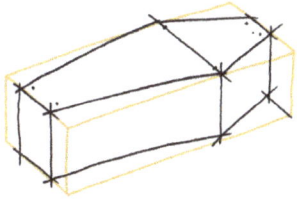
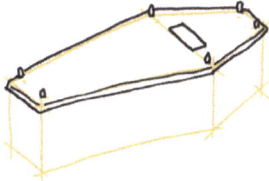

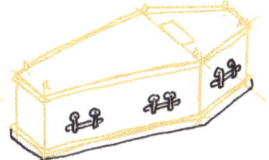

CASKET

1. First, sketch a box for an outline plan, then draw three curves and two lines to make top lid.

2. Draw the edges of the lid.

3. Draw vertical lines to create the sides and draw handles.

4. Finish up by drawing the bottom moulding.

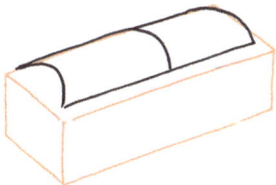
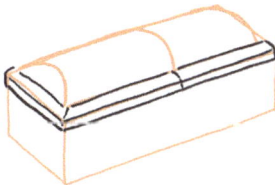
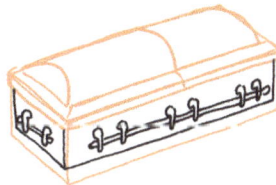
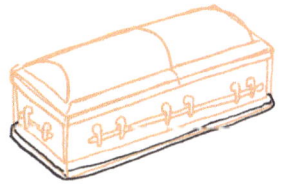

MAUSOLEUM

CLASSICAL STYLE MAUSOLEUM

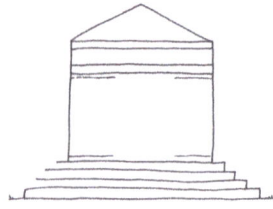

IN MEMORIAM

1782

1. Sketch the outline plan in pencil.

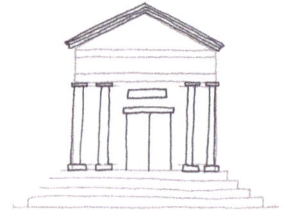

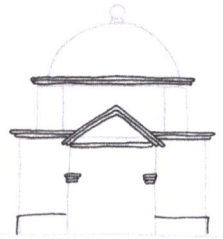

2. Draw the apex of roof, doors, date panel and columns.

3. Draw pattern in pediment, alcoves and door windows

4. Finish with pediment decoration and column flutes.

DOMED MAUSOLEUM

·1392·

1. Sketch the outline plan in pencil.

2. Draw the pediment above doors and all horizontals.

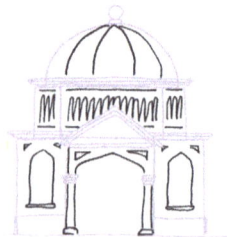

3. Draw sections of dome, door columns, alcoves and pattern.

4. Finish with door, date on pediment and shell pattern in alcoves.

ANGEL SKULL

1. Sketch the skull and cross-bones in pencil first. 2. Then draw the outline of the wings. 3. Draw the individual feathers on the wings in ink, then, 4. Finish with skull detail and shading.

R.I.P.

1. Draw the basic shapes in pencil. 2. Draw around the outline in ink then, 3. Draw the 3d effect on the side of stone and sketch the in-line pattern on the front.
4, Finish with Angel Skull and lettering.

PLAIN & SIMPLE

1. Draw the basic shape in pencil. 2. Draw around the outline in ink.3. Draw the 3d effect on the side of stone and draw lettering then, 4, Finish with shell pattern and shading..

LEANING OVER

1. Draw the basic shape in pencil then 2. Draw around the outline in ink. 3. Draw the 3d effect on the side of stone and sketch the in-line pattern on the front then,
4, Finish with shell pattern and lettering.

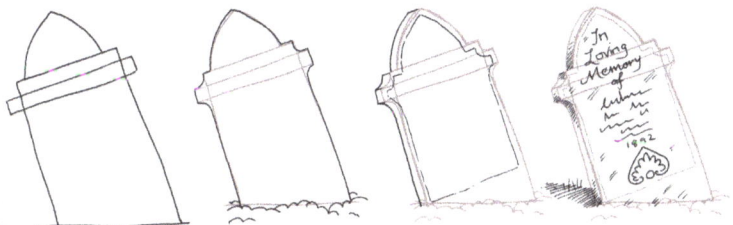

Flicker

1. First draw simple letters in pencil. 2. Then draw an outline, keeping an equal distance all the way around from the pencil letter. 3. Draw the scratchy, flickery outline and erase the pencil. To finish, add flicker lines.

Flicker   Flicker   Flicker

Aa Bb Cc Dd Ee Ff Gg Hh Ii Jj Kk Ll Mm
Nn Oo Pp Qq Rr Ss Tt Uu Vv Ww Xx Yy Zz

BLOB

1. First draw simple letters in pencil. 2. Then draw an outline in pencil, keeping an equal distance all the way around from the pencil letter. 3. Finally, ink the outline with a wobbly line, making it blobby on the bottom. Erase pencil lines.

BLOB   BLOB   BLOB

A B C D E F G H I J K L M N
O P Q R S T U V W X Y Z

SCRATCH

1. First draw simple letters in pencil, making different sizes and angles. 2. Then draw the letter with two, scratchy lines. 3. Finally, add the serifs, or cross pieces with two short strokes. Erase pencil lines and finish with scratch lines.

SCRATCH   SCRATCH   SCRATCH

ABCDEFGHIJKLMNOPQRSTUVWXYZ

LETTERING

SPIRIT

1. First draw simple letters in pencil. 2. Then draw an outline, keeping an equal distance all the way around from the pencil letter. 3. Draw the scratchy, flickery serifs at ends of letter strokes. To finish, erase pencil and add flicker lines.

SPIRIT   SPIRIT   SPIRIT

ABCDEFGHIJKLMNOPQRSTUVWXYZ

GRAVE

1. First draw the outlines for the graves. 2. Sketch the simple letters on the graves in pencil. 3. Then draw an outline, keeping an equal distance all the way around from the pencil letter. 3. Draw the 3d sides of the graves. Finish with shadow and stone texture.

GRAVE   GRAVE

ABCDEFGHIJKLMN
OPQRSTUVWXYZ

SPIDER

1. First draw simple letters in pencil. 2. Then draw the letters in ink with a thin, wobbly line. 3. Draw the curly serifs on the ends of letter strokes and decorate with spider webs. Finish by erasing the pencil lines.

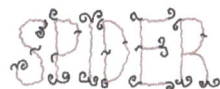

SPIDER   SPIDER   SPIDER

ABCDEFGHIJKLMNOPQRSTUVWXYZ

MUMMY

MUMMY HEAD

1. First draw a simple head outline in pencil.

2. Next, draw first three bandages, plus eye and mouth in ink.

3. Draw the rest of the bandages and draw teeth.

4 Finish with shading and bandage material texture.

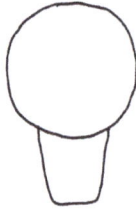   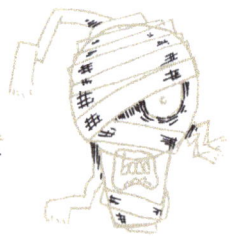

MARAUDING MUMMY

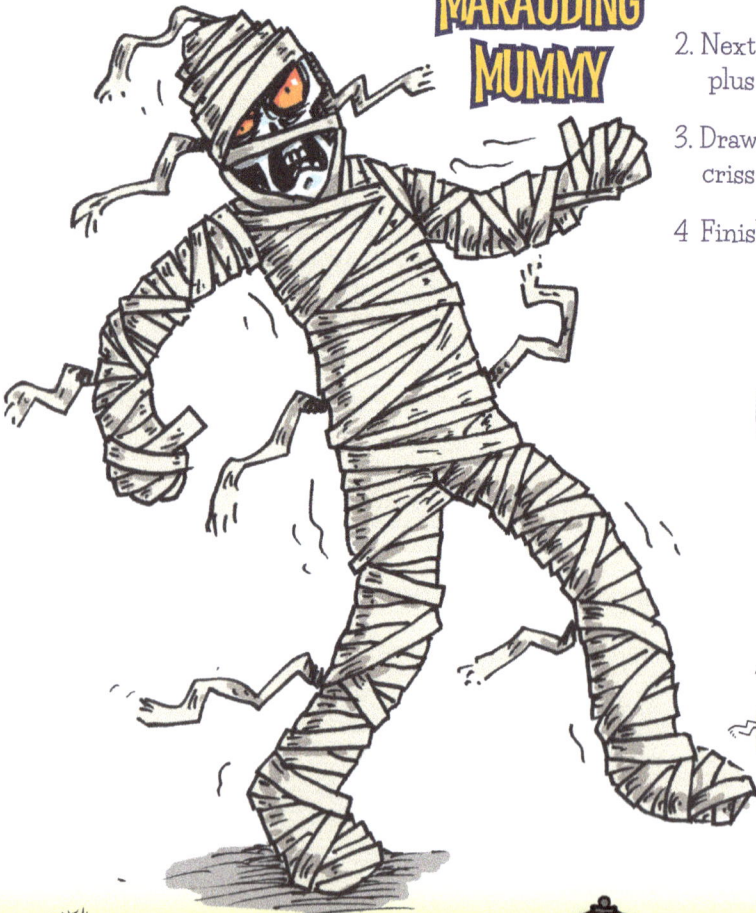

1. First draw a simple body outline in pencil.

2. Next, draw criss-cross bandages, plus eyes and mouth in ink.

3. Draw teeth and bandages between criss-crossed bandages.

4 Finish remaining bandages and add shading.

DRACULA

THE FACE OF DRACULA

1. First draw a simple head outline in pencil.

2. Next, draw hair eyebrows and ears in ink

3. Draw braid around collar, eyes, nose and open mouth.

4 Finish by filling in the hair - then add fangs, and shading.

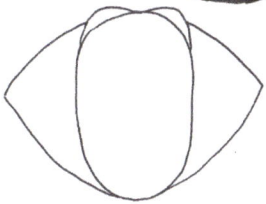

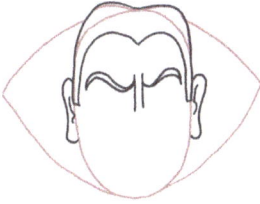

DRACULA'S CLOAK

1. First draw a simple head outline in pencil.

2. Next, draw hair, ears and cloak in ink.

3. Draw face and waistcoat.

4 Finish with hair fangs and shading.

CREATURES OF THE NIGHT

VICIOUS VAMPIRE BAT

1. First draw a simple outline in pencil.
2. Draw inner ears, body, face, legs, tail and top edge of wing in ink
3. Draw outer ears, wing and claws. 4 Finish with fur and shading.

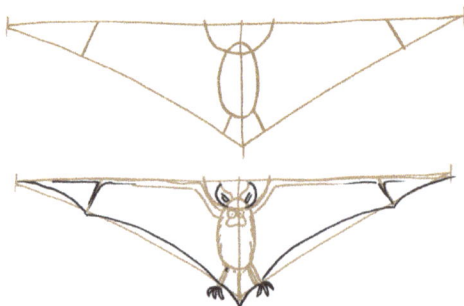
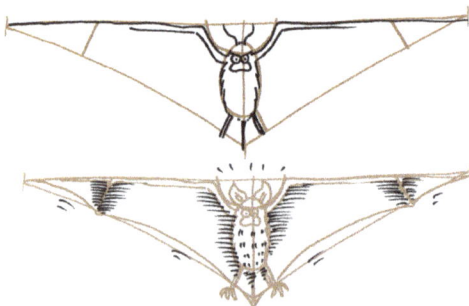

YOMPING YETI

1. First draw a simple outline in pencil.

2. Next, draw fur outline in ink.

3. Draw face and snow.

4 Finish with fur, teeth and tongue.

CREATURES OF THE NIGHT

WAILING WEREWOLF

1. First draw simple outline shapes in pencil.

2. Next, draw face, claws and bottom of feet.

3. Draw the fur outline and top of first claw on feet.

4 Finish with fur effect and rest of claws.

CREATURES OF THE NIGHT

ZANY ZOMBIE

1. First draw simple outline shapes in pencil.

2. Draw hair and face outline and clothes in ink.

3. Draw face details, arms and shoes.

4 Finish with shading and shaky lines.

GRUESOME OGRE

1. Sketch simple outline shapes in pencil.

2. Next, draw clothes, thumb and handle of club.

3. Draw face details, hands, feet and club.

4 Finish with shading and shaky lines.

CREATURES OF THE NIGHT

The Grim Reaper

1. Sketch simple outline shapes in pencil.

2. Draw Cowl, hands and scythe in ink.

3. Draw face details, and ragged clothing.

4 Finish with shading and shaky lines.

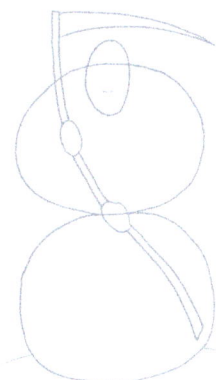

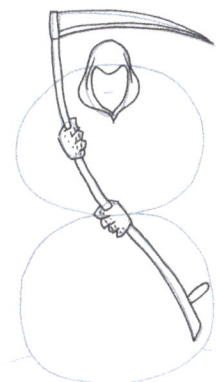

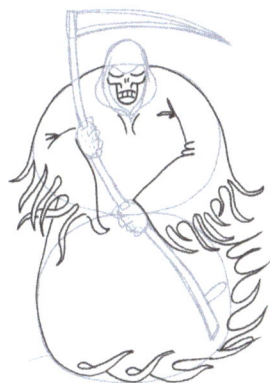

HALLOWEEN MASKS

MEASURE YOUR MASK

Put your thumb on your mouth and a finger on each eye.
Remove hand and place it in the middle of a piece of paper.
Draw around fingers and thumb to mark where to cut out mouth and eye holes.

Choose card to draw mask on.

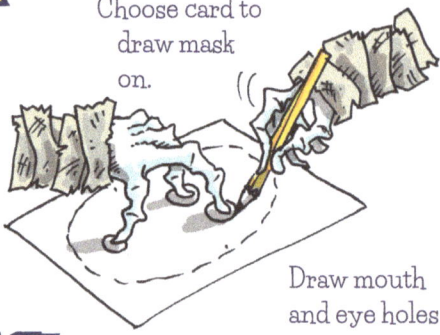

Draw mouth and eye holes

DESIGN YOUR MASK

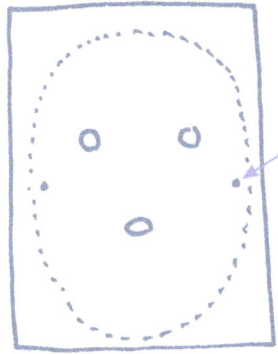

Marks for elastic tie holes.

Make sure mouth and eye holes are placed in pupils and dark, open mouth.

Sketch an outline of the face with eyes and mouth in centre. Mark where holes go on each side.
Plan your design so mouth and eye holes are placed in eyeballs and open mouth. Draw and colour design.

Carefully cut out the mask.

Put card over plasticine or blue tack and punch hole with pencil.

Tie string or elastic through holes on each side.

Your mask is ready to wear.

Download, cut out and wear these masks!

https://bit.ly/DSREMasks

30

HALLOWEEN MASKS

Copy this mask
or download it from
https://bit.ly/DSREMasks

See Mummy
Head design
on page 24.

31

FLY BY NIGHTS

DEATH'S HEAD MOTH

1. First draw simple outline plan in pencil.

2. Ink the body and head and outline the top and bottom edges of the wings.

3. Draw the outline of the death's head, antennae and legs. Draw body stripes and lower wing veins.

4. Finish by filling in black areas and decorate the wings.

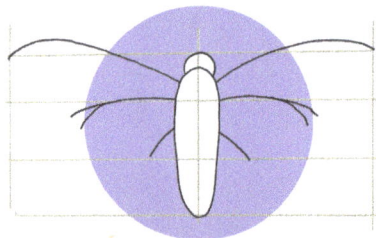

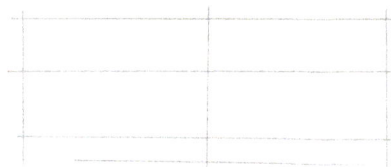

ODD BALL OWL

1. First draw simple outline shapes in pencil.

2. In ink, draw body outline, tail, beak and lower eyebrow.

3. Draw wings and tail detail, then the upper part of eyebrow. Then draw eyes underneath.

4. Finish with feather details and shading around the eyes.

ARACHNIA!

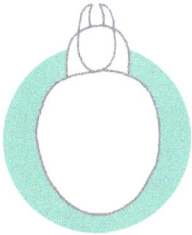

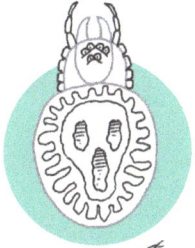

SCREAMING SPIDER

1. Draw the body outline in ink.

2. Draw pedipalps, eyes, leg joints and screaming body pattern

3. Draw eight legs.

4. Add shading and make your spider spooky, spiky and hairy!

TANGLED WEB

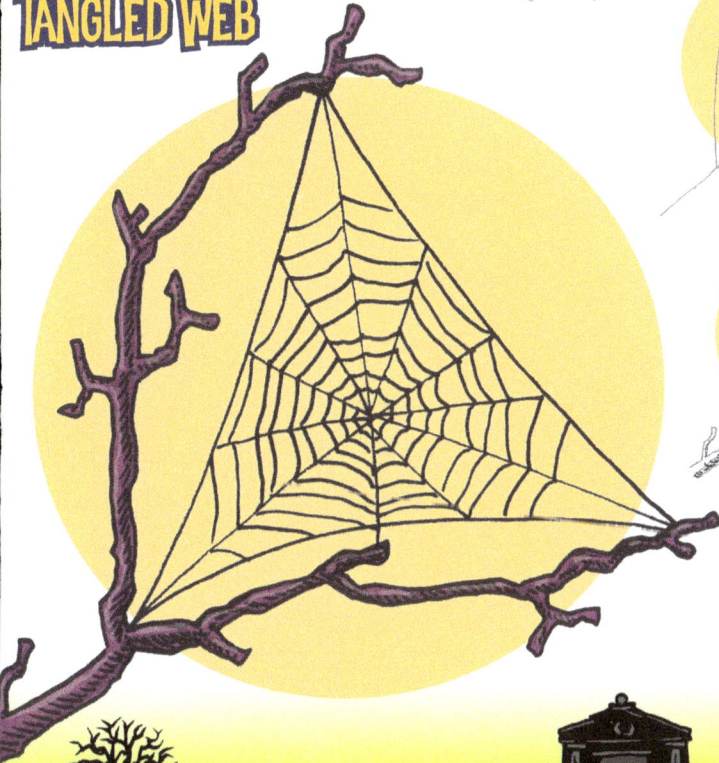

1. Sketch tree and web outline in pencil.

2. Draw Tree and web in ink.

3. Complete web sections and shade tree.

4. Draw the spiral on the web.

NIGHT LIGHTS

DRIPPING CANDLE

1. Sketch the outline of the candle in pencil

2. Draw the flame and soft waxy top.

3. Draw wax dripping down side of candle

4. Draw another stream of wax behind the first drip.

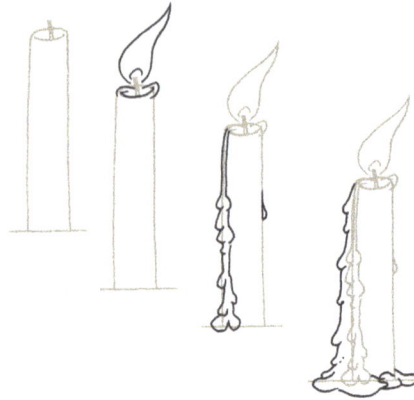
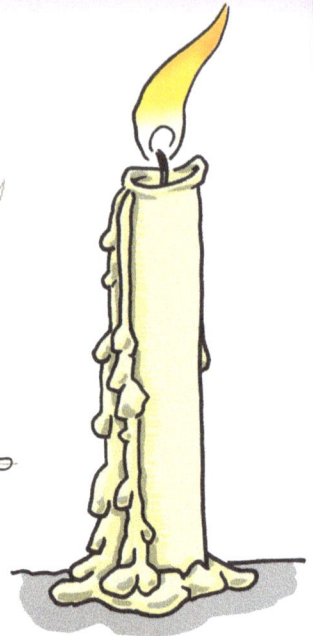

LUMINOUS LANTERN

1. Sketch the outline of the lantern in pencil

2. Ink the metal parts of the lantern.

3. Draw the candle inside the lantern with flame and dripping wax.

4. Add shading to the lantern and candle.

CRYSTAL BALL

1. Sketch the outline of the crystal ball in pencil

2. Ink the glass ball.

3. Draw the base.

4. Add shading and high lights.

IN THE DARK FOREST

SCARY TREE

1. Sketch a plan of the tree in pencil. 2. Ink in the "eyebrows, arms and mouth to give a 3d effect.

3. Draw the top branches. 4. Draw leaves on the ends of branches and finish with shading.

HAUNTED TOWN

Silhouettes are a great way to create spooky looking drawings.

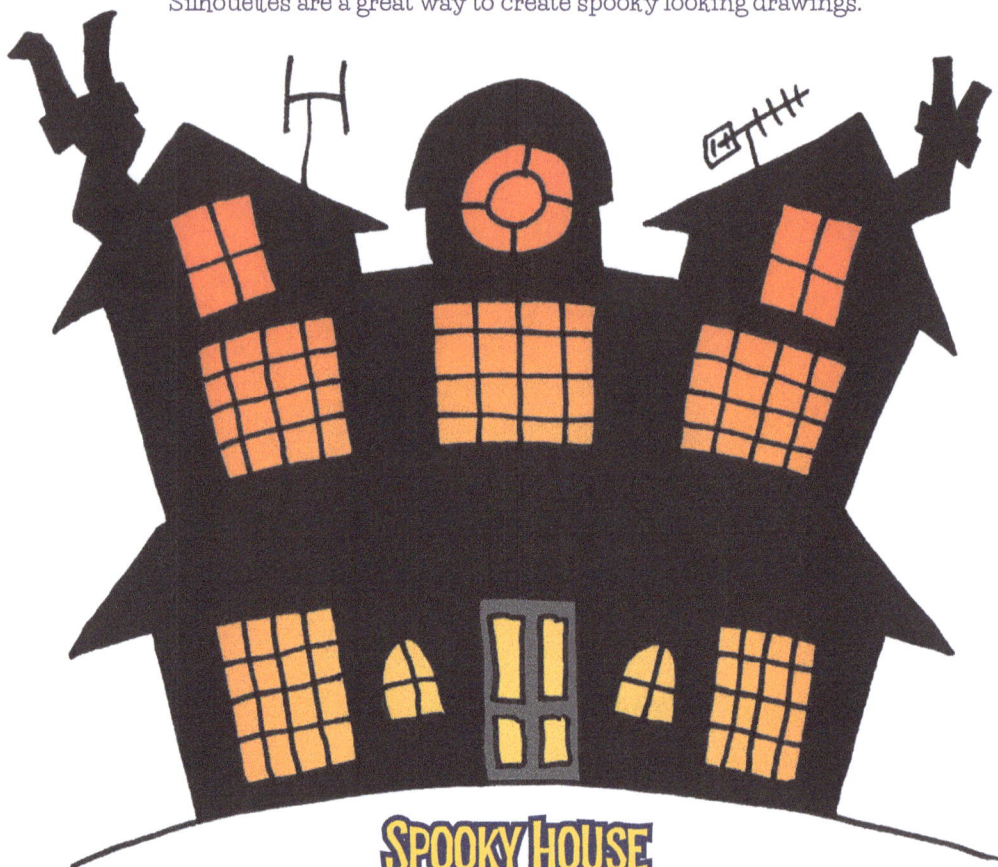

SPOOKY HOUSE

1. Draw the outline of the house.

2. Draw the outlines of the window frames.

3. Draw the middle cross-frames in the windows and roof over central curved section.

4. Finish windows and draw wonky chimneys and TV aerials.

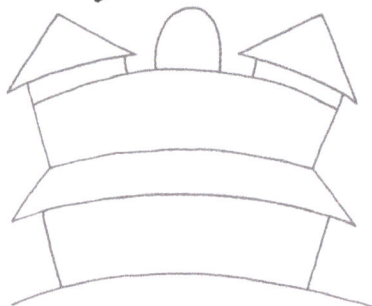

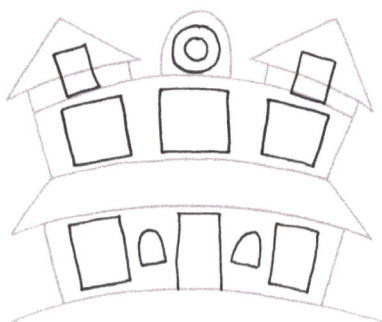

CREEPY CASTLE

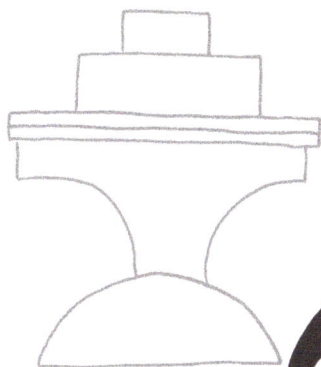

1. Sketch the outlines of the castle in pencil.

2. In ink, draw the battlements, flags and base outline of the castle.

3. Draw the four towers and add conical roofs. Then draw all the windows.

4. Finish off by drawing the zig-zag lines where the high lights will be, before inking in the rest of the castle, to create the silhouette effect.

NIGHT CRAWLERS

SLITHERING SLUG

1. Sketch the outlines of the slug in pencil.

2. In ink, draw the slime, horns and mouth.

3. Draw the body and eye-stalks.

4. Finish off with eyeballs, stripes and shading.

PUTRID PILL BUG

1. Sketch the outline in pencil.

2. In ink, draw scales.

3. Draw eyes mouth and antennae.

4. Finish off with legs.

MORBID MAGGOT

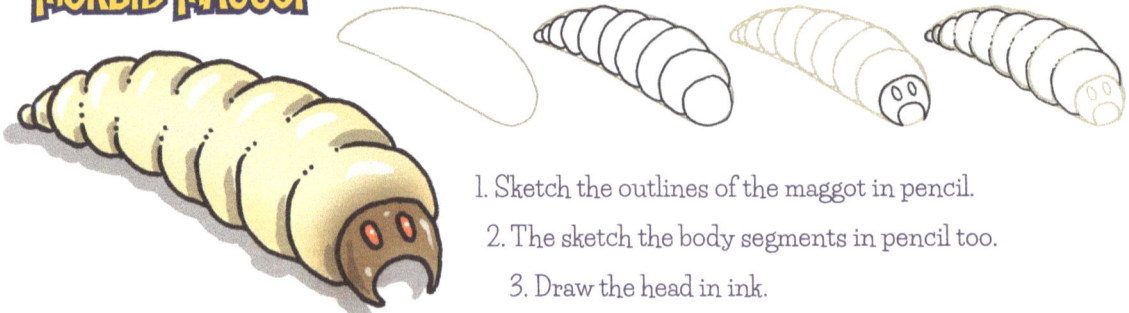

1. Sketch the outlines of the maggot in pencil.

2. The sketch the body segments in pencil too.

3. Draw the head in ink.

4. Finish off the body segments in ink.

MALICIOUS MILLIPEDE

1. Sketch the outlines of the millipede in pencil.

2. Draw the head and tail in ink.

3. Draw the body segments.

4. Finish off by drawing all the legs.

SCARY SALLY SCARECROW

1. Sketch the outline shapes in pencil.

2. In ink, draw the face and headband.

3. Draw the dress and flowers in hair.

4. Finish with dress pattern, stick and straw hands.

THE NIGHT WATCHMAN

1. Sketch the outline shapes in pencil. 2. In ink, draw the hat, hair and jacket lapels. 3. Draw the face, coat, collar and tie and finish the jacket and trousers. 4. Finish the drawing with shading and straw hands and feet.

BAWLING BOB THE CRAZY CORN COB

1. Sketch the outline shapes in pencil. 2. In ink, draw the leaves around the cob. 3. Draw the eyes, teeth and tongue. 4. Finish with shading on leaves and by drawing kernels around the face to make a mouth.

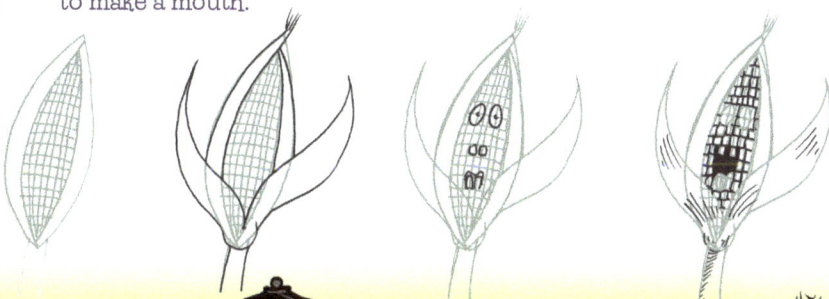

BRAINS

BRAINS ON A PLATE

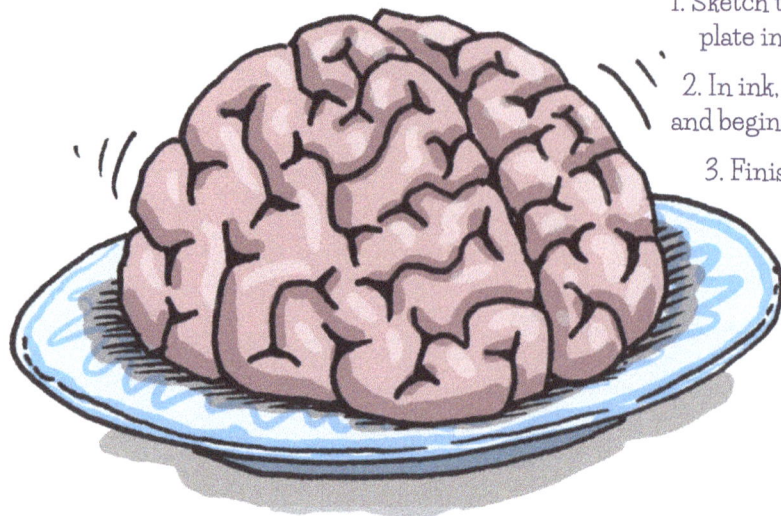

1. Sketch the outlines of the brains and plate in pencil.

2. In ink, draw the outline of the brain and begin to draw the folds.

3. Finish drawing the folds in the spaces left in between outside folds.

4. Finish off with shading and wobble lines.

 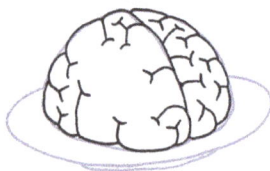 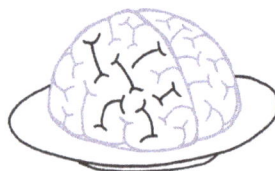 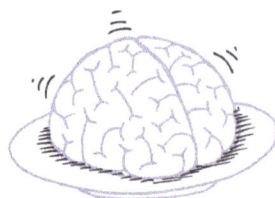

BRAINS IN A JAR

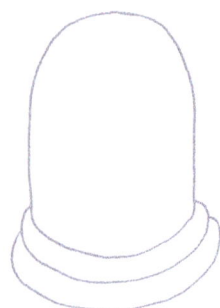 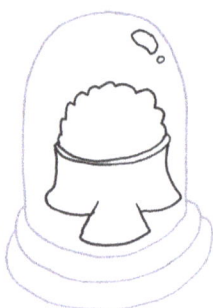

 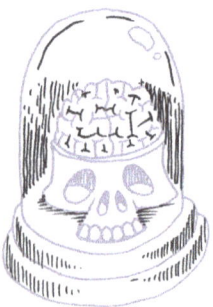

1. Sketch the outlines of the glass dome.

2. In ink, draw the brain and skull outline and add shiny high light.

3. Draw eyes, nose and teeth and first layer of brain folds.

4. Draw the inner brain folds and finish with shading.

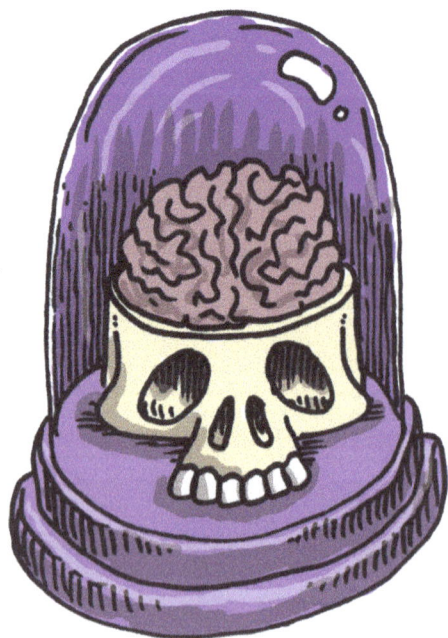

CALAVERA – MEXICAN SUGAR SKULL

Calavera or Mexican Sugar Skulls are given as gifts on the Día de Muertas, or Day of the Dead, at Halloween.

1. Sketch the outlines of the skull, eyes, heart-shaped nose and smile for mouth.

2. In ink, draw the draw circles for the eyeballs and centre of forehead flower.

Draw teardrops for nostrils and semicircles for centres of the rest of the flowers on theedge of skull. Draw the teeth.

3. Draw flower petals and branch on forehead. Draw "frilly" edges to eyes, nose and chin.

4. Finish off with shading on petals. Draw leaves on stalks, curly patterns and place small circles inside the "frills".

This is also available as a print out mask - see page 30.

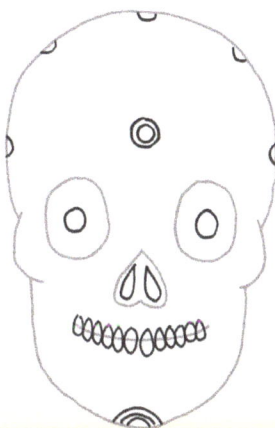

TRICK OR TREAT!

CAT GIRL

1. Sketch the outlines first.   2. Draw hair, ears, bib and tail in ink, .   3. Draw face, hands and buttons on bib.
4. Finish with the lantern and laces on shoes.

PUMPKIN BOY

1. Sketch the pumpkin outlines first.
2. Draw hat, arms and legs in ink.
3. Draw face.   4. Finish with the face on the pumpkin.

BAT GIRL

1. Sketch the face and bat wing outlines first.
2. Draw ears, legs and shoes in ink.
3. Draw face.
4. Finish with hands and candy bucket.

DINO BOY

1. Sketch the dinosaur outlines first.
2. Draw dino eyes, spine and legs in ink.
3. Draw boy's face in dino mouth.
4. Finish with hands and candy bucket.

42

DEVIL BOY

1. Sketch the outlines first.
2. Draw feet, hands and candy bucket in ink.
3. Draw boy's face, hood and horns.
4. Finish with pitchfork, chest emblem and tail.

FAIRY GIRL

1. Sketch the fairy outlines first. 2. Draw hair and face, magic wand and skirt in ink. 3. Draw the wings behind the body. 4. Finish with pattern on wings and skirt.

SPIDER BOY

1. Sketch the spider outlines first. 2. Draw hat with eyes and pincers, head and inner body, in ink. 3. Draw boy's face and six legs. 4. Finish by adding stripes to arms and legs.

WITCH GIRL

1. Sketch face hat brim and dress outlines first.
2. Draw hat, hair and hands in ink.
3. Draw face, broomstick and dress.
4. Finish with legs and lace on dress.

HALLOWEEN

CANDY BUCKET

1. Sketch the bucket outlines in pencil first.
2. Draw the inner mouth of the bucket and top handle in ink.
3. Draw lower side of handle and rest of bucket.
4. Finish with the bucket face, candy and highlight on handle.

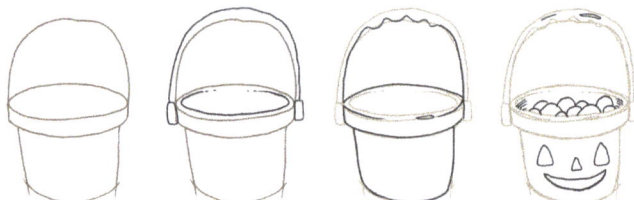

GHUMMY WORMS

1. Sketch a curvy centre line in pencil first.
2. Draw the top of the worm in ink.
3. Draw lower side of worm.
4. Finish with segment lines.

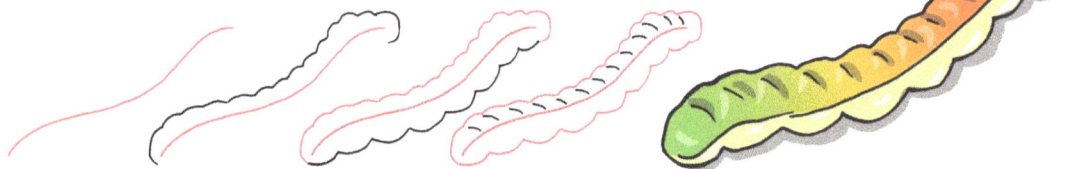

JELLY BEANS

1. Sketch three curving lines from a centre point in pencil.
2. Draw the beans in ink, to fit around curves.
3. Draw shading.
4. Finish with highlights on beans.

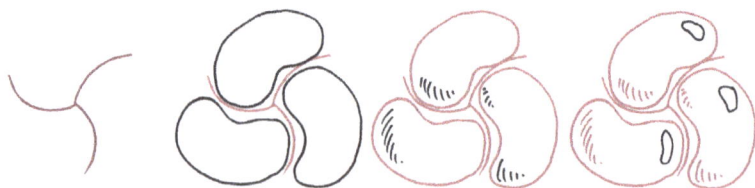

LOLLY POPS

1. Sketch a circle in pencil first.
2. Draw curvy cross in ink.
3. Draw another curvy cross and stick.
4. Finish with shading.

CANDY STORE

GHUMMY GHOUL

1. Sketch a teardrop shape in pencil.
2. Draw the wobbly ghost outline in ink.
3. Draw the eyes.   4. Finish with shading.

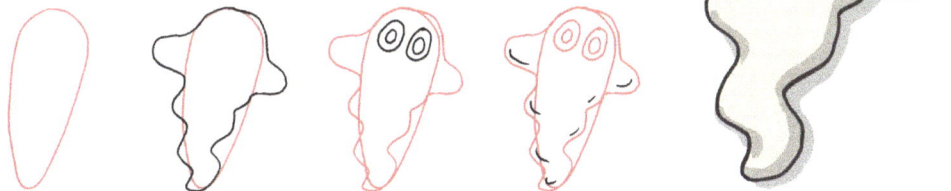

HALLOWEEN SURPRISE

1. Sketch circle and two triangles in pencil.
2. Draw wrapper pattern in ink.
3. Draw wrapper end-twists.
4. Finish with shading and highlights.

LIQUORICE SKULL

1. Draw a circle in ink, and another inside it.
2. Draw two lines at a shallow angle.
3. Join the lines with a curve.
4. Finish with skull in inner circle.

TOFFEE APPLE

1. Draw a circle in ink.
2. Draw stick in apple top.
3. Draw apple outline, break up the line at the bottom.
4. Finish with dripping toffee and highlights.

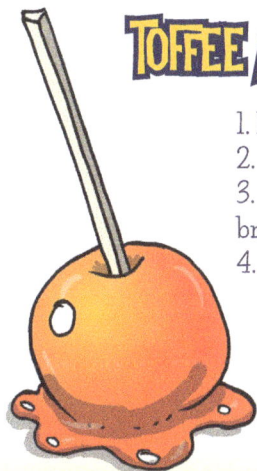

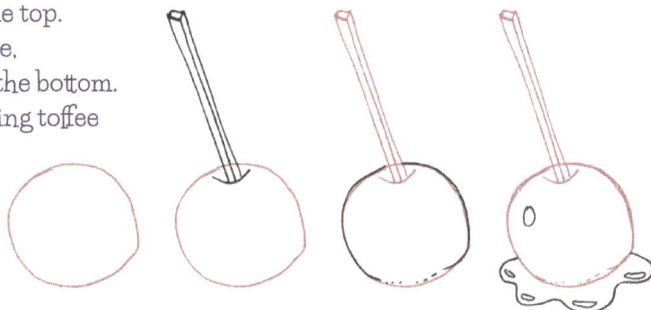

CREEPIES

CREEPY CLOWN

1. Sketch the creepy clown's outlines first. 2. Draw hair face, bow tie and shoes in ink. 3. Draw jacket shorts and braces. 4. Finish with pattern on shorts, flower, buttons and patchwork pieces.

ZOM-BABY

1. Sketch the baby's outlines first. 2. Draw face outline and zombie romper suit in ink. 3. Draw face, hands, feet and buttons. 4. Finish with shadows, scratches and zombie-baby hypno-marks.

THE ANGEL OF DEATH

1. Sketch the angel's outlines first. 2. Draw hair and dress outline in ink. 3. Draw face, dress details and wings behind dress. 4. Finish with hands, feet and feathers on wings.

THE END!

ZOMBIE HAND

1. Sketch basic outlines in pencil first.

2. Draw stitches and outline of lower hand in ink.

3. Draw shadows on stitches and severed hand wound under stitches.

4. Finish with shading and zombie wobble lines.

THE MUMMY SPEAKS!

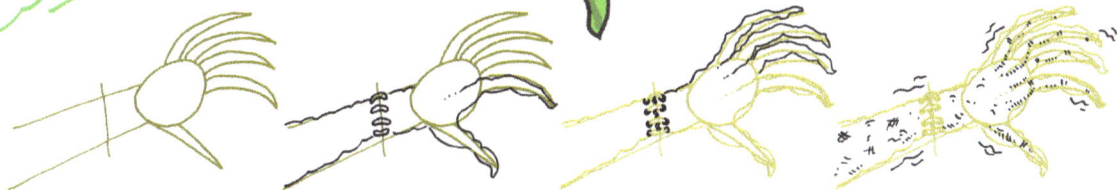

1. Sketch the outlines of the hand in pencil first. 2. Draw top bandages on thumb and arm in ink. 3. Draw the pencil and bandages behind it. Then draw the bandages under top bandages on arm and thumb. 4. Finish with hands, feet and feathers on wings.

www.ingramcontent.com/pod-product-compliance
Lightning Source LLC
Chambersburg PA
CBHW041434040426
42452CB00021B/2974